The Aust
Seven

CW01645821

Anita Jackson

WITHDRAWN

10070

Stanley Thornes (Publishers) Ltd

© ILEA 1974

All rights reserved. No part of this publication may be reproduced or transmitted in any form or by any means, electronic or mechanical, including photocopy, recording, or any information storage and retrieval system, without permission in writing from the publisher or under licence from the Copyright Licensing Agency Limited. Further details of such licences (for reprographic reproduction) may be obtained from the Copyright Licensing Agency Limited, of 90 Tottenham Court Road, London W1P 9HE.

First published in 1976 by Hutchinson Education in association with the Inner London Education Authority Media Resources Centre
Reprinted in 1977, 1979, 1981, 1983, 1984, 1986, 1988, 1989

Reprinted in 1992 by
Stanley Thornes (Publishers) Ltd
Old Station Drive
Leckhampton
CHELTENHAM GL53 0DN
England

ISBN 0 7487 1042 6

WEST SUSSEX LIBRARIES

Copy No.		Class No. F	
Supplier	Cromwell	Date Invoiced 3.3.93	
1st Loc.	Initials	2nd Loc.	Initials
3rd Loc.	Initials	4th Loc.	Initials

Cover photograph by Neill Bruce
Cover design by Martin Grant-Hudson
Printed and bound in Great Britain at Martin's of Berwick

1

I used to love sport. Any kind of sport. Football, cricket, tennis, darts – you name it, I did it. I was never the sort of person to sit about much. I always wanted to be up and about. I used to do a lot of gardening as well. That's all over now. I can't even play darts. I just sit in my wheelchair and look out of the window.

I can see the grass in the garden getting longer every day but I can't do anything about it. I broke my back in the accident and now my legs are no good. They won't move at all. They just hang down in front of me.

I can't get out of the wheelchair on my own. At night, my wife, May, has to lift me out of the chair. I can't do anything on my own. I can't even go to the lavatory on my own. May makes a joke of it but there isn't much to laugh at. I'm helpless now and I've just got to face it. I'll be in this chair for the rest of my life.

I can't use my legs but I can still use my hands. At first my hands were too weak to hold a cup but now I can feed myself. I can hold a newspaper and I can play cards. My hands are strong enough to do that. I can write as well. I can hold a pen and I can write.

It isn't easy. The pen in my hand is shaking. My arm is stiff and my writing is untidy but I will not give up. I will keep writing because I must tell someone what happened to me. I must write my story down. I hope that someone will read it and believe it.

My wife tells everyone that I had an accident in the car. She tells them that one dark night, the car skidded and I crashed into a tree. In a way she is right. It was a dark night and I did crash into a tree, but it was *not* an accident.

I told my wife what really happened but she didn't believe me. I can't blame her. If someone told me the story, I don't think I would believe it. I'm just an ordinary sort of chap. I didn't believe in ghosts. 'Ghosts!' I used to say, 'I don't believe in all that rubbish.' I know better now.

I didn't get into this wheelchair by accident. Someone or something put me here. Was it a ghost? Was it a spirit? You can call it what you like. I say it was a ghost. I don't like the word 'ghost' but it's the best word I can think of. I will tell you what happened and you can make up your own mind.

You may think I'm mad. You may put this book down and say, 'Poor chap, the accident must have done something to his mind.' Maybe I *am* mad. I don't know any more. But I want to tell you what happened. I want to write it all down, just as it happened. All you have to do is read it and make up your own mind.

Was it a ghost? Was it? The car was real. The crash was real. This wheelchair is real and I am real. Those are the facts. Don't forget that. Now I'll tell you the rest. I'll tell you everything that happened.

2

Last year, about the middle of June, I decided to buy a car. I didn't really need a car. I had an old van and it was still going well so I didn't want to sell it. It had my name, Edward Brown, painted on both sides. The paint was peeling off.

My wife May kept saying to me, 'Ed, why don't you get rid of that old van and buy a new car? It would be really nice to have a proper car.' I didn't fancy a new car but she kept on at me, and so I sort of gave in. I said, 'O.K. May, I'll tell you what I'll do. I won't get a new car but I'll get a good secondhand one. Something smart. How about that?'

May was pleased. She hated my old van. Women always sum up a car by the way it looks. My van looked a mess. May wanted to go to the second-hand car place down the road. It's a big place just a few minutes walk from our house, but I wouldn't go. I know the people down there. A lot of crooks. I said to May, 'If you want to give your money away, that's the place to go. They rob you blind.'

I told May that I would look in the local paper. There are always plenty of cars for sale. You just have to look at the adverts. If you get a car that way, you cut out the middle man. Car dealers are always looking for a quick profit.

I got the local paper and sat looking at the list of cars for sale. May came and peered over my shoulder. 'Look Ed! How about that one?' she said. The advert said: ROVER 2000, 1971, WHITE WITH RED UPHOLSTERY, £900.

'You must be joking,' I said to May. 'I'm not going to pay more than £500.' May kept on reading out the adverts, and I kept on shaking my head and saying no. I had seen an advert down at the bottom of the list. It seemed to stand out on the page. I looked at May but I could see that she hadn't even noticed it.

May's voice went on and on but I wasn't listening. My eyes kept going back to the small advert at the bottom of the page. It said: AUSTIN 7, 1928, PERFECT CONDITION. RING 01-787 8602.

'How about this Morris?' said May. 'What Morris?' I asked. May walked crossly over to the window. 'Edward Brown,' she said, 'you haven't been listening to me. I don't think you want to buy a car. I think you want to keep your dirty old van.' But May was wrong. I did want a car. Not any old car. I wanted that old Austin 7.

Don't ask me why I wanted it. I don't know. I didn't say anything about it to May. I knew she wouldn't understand. She wanted a new car, and I was dying to get my hands on an old Austin 7. I waited until she had gone out, then I rang the number in the advert. As I picked up the 'phone my hands were shaking. It might have gone. It might be sold already. I wanted that car – really wanted it.

'Hello,' I said. 'Am I speaking to the owner of the Austin 7?' A woman's voice said, 'Just a minute. I'll get my husband. It was his car.' Her voice sounded sad, and there was something odd about what she said. Why did she say it *was* his car. Had he sold it already?

I waited a long time, then a man spoke to me. The car was still there. It hadn't gone. I asked him how much he wanted for it. '£900' he said. I almost dropped the phone. What a stupid price! £900 for an old Austin 7! I should have put the phone down, but I didn't.

Suddenly I found myself saying, 'I'll come round and have a look at it. Will you give me your name and address?' The man told me his name and I wrote it down in my notebook. Edward Kelly, 52 Elm Road. I knew how to get there. 'My name is Brown.' I said.

I was just going to put the phone down, when he said an odd thing. 'You must be called Edward,' he said. I was a bit surprised. 'Yes, that's right,' I said. 'Edward. My friends call me Ed.' Very softly he said, 'That's my name too.' He didn't say another word. The phone gave a click and he was gone.

3

The next day I went to see the Austin 7. 'Where are you going?' asked May. She could see me putting my coat on. 'I'm going down to the sports club for a game of tennis,' I said. It was a lie. I don't usually lie to May. I should have told her the truth, but the words just slipped out. 'I wonder why I said that?' I thought, then I went out of the front door.

I got into my old van and drove to 52 Elm Road. Mrs Kelly saw me walking up her path and she came out to meet me. Her hands were wet. She must have been doing some washing. 'I've come about the Austin 7,' I told her. She smiled at me. 'Come round to the side of the house,' she said. 'My husband is sitting out in the sun. He is waiting for you.'

I followed Mrs Kelly along the path. As we walked round to the side of the house, I saw the car. The little Austin 7. The sight of it made my heart jump. It was beautiful. It was perfect. The body work was black and gleaming and the headlamps were shining. It looked brand new. It was made in 1928, but it looked brand new. I was amazed.

Slowly, I went across the grass to the car and put my hand on the bonnet. I ran my hand gently over the paintwork. It felt as smooth as silk. There wasn't a mark on it. Not a dent. Not a scratch. It was perfect.

'Do you like it, Mr Brown?' said a man's voice. I turned round and saw a man in a wheelchair. His face was thin and pale, and his legs were covered with a blanket. 'I am Edward Kelly,' he said.

I shook hands with him. Poor fellow. He could hardly lift his arm. I wondered if he had been in a wheelchair all his life. No, he must have had an accident. The Austin 7 was his. Once upon a time he must have been able to drive it.

Edward Kelly could see that I was mad about the car. He knew I would pay £900 for it. Maybe you think I was a fool to pay so much, but I wanted that car. I wanted it more than anything in the world. 'Try it,' said Mr Kelly. 'Take it for a little run.'

I got into the car and went for a short drive. It ran beautifully. The engine made a noise like a happy cat. Everything was perfect. The car felt as if it had been made for me. I had to buy it. I didn't waste time. I drove back to Mr Kelly's house and paid him £900.

He had got a good price for the car but he didn't look very pleased. His face was sad and he kept looking at me in an odd way. I chatted to him for a while, but he didn't have much to say for himself. He seemed to have something on his mind. Just for something to say, I started to talk about the sports club. Mr Kelly gave a little smile. 'I used to be keen on football,' he said. 'Of course that was before I had the accident.'

It was getting late. I was longing to step into the Austin 7 and drive it home. 'I must be going now,' I said to Mr Kelly. 'Won't you stay and have some tea?' he asked. I shook my head. 'No thank you. I must get home. My wife will be waiting for me.'

Just as I was going to walk away from him, he shot out his hand and grabbed my arm. 'Are you sure about this?' he said. His face was pale and he looked as if he was going to cry. In a low voice he said, 'You don't have to buy the car. I'll give you the money back if you like. If you don't want the Austin, just say so.'

I was a bit surprised. He seemed sorry to get rid of the car. 'I want it,' I said. 'I'm quite sure about it. Goodbye, Mr Kelly, and thank you.'

4

When I got home May was waiting for me. She saw me park the Austin outside our house. 'Where is the van?' she asked. 'Not very far away,' I said. 'I shall go and get it tomorrow.' May looked at the Austin. 'Why were you driving that odd looking thing? Who does it belong to?'

I had to tell her the truth but I knew she wouldn't like it. 'It's an Austin 7,' I told her. 'It was made in 1928. It's a pretty rare car. You don't see many of them about.' May stood there with a frown on her face. She was waiting for me to tell her the rest. 'It's mine,' I said. 'I've just bought it.'

May was wild. 'That thing!' she said. 'Don't tell me you went out and spent money on that thing. We need a proper car. You must be mad, Ed.' I began to get cross. Pretty soon we were having a row. A really big row. It ended with May in tears. She said that she would never set foot in the Austin. Never.

At the time I didn't think she meant it. I thought that she would get used to the car. Even if she didn't like the Austin, I thought she would ride in it. I was wrong. May didn't ever go near the car. She didn't ever step inside it. Not once. When I went out in the Austin 7, I always went alone.

5

When I'd had the car for about six weeks I began to think that there was something odd about it. Something I didn't understand. It isn't easy to put this into words. At first I just had an odd feeling when I was in the car. I felt as if I was closed in. The inside of the car seemed very hot and stuffy. I used to open all the windows to let the fresh air in.

At first I wasn't worried. After all, it was the middle of summer. Cars often get hot and stuffy in the summer. You just have to put up with it. That is what I told myself. Then I noticed that I *always* needed to open the windows. Even late at night. Even on cold wet days. The inside of the car was always stuffy. There was always an odd smell.

A smell. Quite a nice smell. What was it? It was very strong. My nose was full of it every time I got into the car. I had to open the windows.

One day I found out what the smell was. It happened like this. I was at work. I was sitting at the desk in my office. There was a knock at the door and a girl came in. She worked in the office next door. Suddenly the room was full of that smell.

The girl walked over to my desk and gave me a pile of papers. 'My boss told me to give you these,' she said. I just sat there sniffing. It was that smell. The smell in the car. 'Do you like my perfume?' she said. 'My boy friend gave it to me. He got it in France. It cost a lot of money.'

So that was it! It was perfume. A woman's perfume. I smiled at the girl. 'It's very nice,' I said. She went out of the office and I sat there thinking hard. Perfume. It wasn't so odd after all. Maybe Mrs Kelly used that perfume. Maybe she spilt some in the Austin. The smell would last for weeks. That was why I could still smell it.

When I got home from work I went into the kitchen. I got a cloth and a bucket of hot water. 'Is that you, Edward?' called May. She was in the living room. 'Yes, dear,' I said. 'What are you doing?' she asked. 'I'm going to clean the inside of the Austin,' I said. 'I'm going to give it a really good clean.'

I got to work. I started with the seats and washed everything. It took me about two hours. When I had finished, the inside of the car was dripping wet. I had to let it dry out, so I left the doors and windows open. It was a hot evening.

Just before it got dark I went out and shut the car. I couldn't leave it open all night.

The inside of the car smelt fresh and clean, and it was almost dry. I had got rid of the perfume. I went to bed feeling pleased with myself.

LIBRARY
MILLAIS SCHOOL
DEPOT ROAD
HORSHAM, SUSSEX

6

I didn't drive the Austin for a few days. May had a bad cold. She was feeling a bit fed up so I spent a lot of time at home. On Monday May was a lot better. Her sister was coming round in the evening and I decided to go to the club. I don't get on with May's sister. To tell you the truth, I can't stand her. I made up my mind to be out of the house before she arrived.

At 6.30 I had a wash and a shave. I was out of the house by 7 o'clock. I opened the door of the Austin and jumped in. The smell hit me at once. That smell. Perfume. It had come back. It was as strong as ever.

I opened all the windows and started the engine. I hoped that the smell would go away. It didn't. It seemed to get stronger and stronger. When I arrived at the club I was glad to get out of the car.

The club was almost empty. I wasn't surprised. It's always a bit quiet on a Monday night. Anyway, I had a game of table tennis then I went to the bar and had a few drinks. I kept thinking about the Austin. Why hadn't the smell gone? Where was it coming from?

I didn't spend long at the club. I wanted to get to bed early so I left at 10.30. I walked out of the club and went towards the car park. It was a fine night. The stars seemed very bright.

The Austin was standing by itself, shining in the moonlight. I ran my hand over the bonnet. It was a beautiful car. I was lucky to get a car like this. A 1928 Austin in perfect condition. It must have been well looked after.

I stepped into the car and drove off. The smell of the perfume filled my nose. It was a sweet smell. It was so strong that it made my head spin. You know what I mean. If you sit next to a woman who is wearing strong perfume, it makes you a bit dizzy. That was how I felt.

The road ahead of me was grey in the moonlight. The engine was humming softly. Then I heard something. I heard someone call my name. Edward. I went cold all over. I looked round at the back seat but there was no one there. Of course there wasn't. I was just being silly. Then I heard it again. 'Edward, Edward,' said a soft voice.

I stopped the car. But the voice didn't stop. It was inside the car. Someone was speaking to me. Someone was calling my name. It was a woman's voice. I sat still, frozen with fear. The voice went on. Soft and low. Yes, it was a woman's voice. It kept saying my name over and over again. Just my name. Edward.

I started the car and drove home at top speed.

7

For a few days I drove my old van. I didn't go out in the Austin. I was afraid to step inside it. Then May asked me about it. 'Why aren't you driving your Austin?' she asked. 'You spent £900 on that thing and now you don't even use it. What a waste of money.'

That made me a bit cross. 'Of course I'm going to use it,' I said. 'It's a beautiful car. That £900 was well spent. The Austin is in perfect condition. I could sell it for £1,000 tomorrow if I wanted to.' May gave a little laugh. 'Well, I wish you would,' she said, 'then we could get a proper car.'

I didn't tell May about the voice. Now that I thought about it, it seemed stupid. A woman's voice in the car. I must have had too much to drink. That was it. I imagined it. I had too much to drink and I imagined it. I decided to forget about it. I had been a fool.

For the rest of the week I was very busy at work. Two of the staff in my office were on holiday and one was off sick. There was a lot of work to be done and I had to get on with it. I was rushed off my feet. I didn't have time to think about the Austin. I drove the van to work and the Austin sat in the garage at home. I almost forgot that it was there.

8

On Friday I had a bit of bad luck. The van broke down. I wasn't really surprised. It had been in a bad state for months. I didn't have time to work on it myself so I had it towed into a garage. May and I were going out that night. Some friends had asked us to go over to their place for dinner. We would have to go in the Austin.

I told May. 'Come on,' I said. 'Don't be silly, May. I know you don't like the Austin but the van is off the road. We will have to go in the Austin.' May started to get upset. 'You can go in the Austin and I'll go on the bus,' she said. 'Now you are being stupid,' I told her.

It was no good. She wouldn't change her mind. She wanted to go on the bus. In the end I let her. I saw her onto the bus then I drove off in the Austin.

The sky was dark and stormy. Rain was beginning to fall. I had only been in the car five minutes when I heard the voice. It was saying my name over and over again. Edward, Edward, Edward. I didn't have far to go, so I put my foot down and drove as fast as I could.

I wasn't imagining it. There really was a voice. A woman's voice. Soft and sad. It was just as if there was a woman in the back seat. But the back seat was dark and empty. I was shaking with fear.

'Who are you?' I said. My mouth was so dry that I could hardly speak. There was no reply. 'Who are you?' I shouted. Still there was no reply. Then the voice began again. 'Edward,' it said to me. 'Dear Edward. Don't hurt me. I still love you. I want to be with you. Edward. Edward.'

'Go away,' I shouted. 'I don't know you. Go away and leave me alone.' I was driving very fast. My hands were gripping the steering wheel. I was cold with fear.

'Dear Edward,' said the voice. 'Why don't you love me any more? You used to love me. You loved me when we went on holiday. You loved me when we went to France. We went in the Austin. Do you remember? That was a good year. 1930 was a good year, Edward.'

I looked up at the mirror. I could see the empty back seat. Where was the voice coming from? Who was it? Why was she talking about 1930? I wasn't alive in 1930. I hadn't even been born.

I turned off the main road. There was the house. My friends' house. At last I could stop the car and get out. Thank God. I pulled into the kerb and turned off the engine. I had got there. Now I could go in and see my friends.

May had got there before me. She was sitting in a chair chatting to our friends. They were happy and smiling. Everything was normal. I felt as if I had just woken up after a bad dream.

Should I tell them about the voice? No, I would wait until I got home, then I would tell May about it. I couldn't talk about it now. They would think that I had gone mad.

I must have looked pale. May said, 'What's the matter, Ed? Are you ill?' 'Oh, it's nothing,' I said. 'I'm not feeling too good. I'll tell you about it later.'

At nine o'clock we sat down to dinner. I couldn't eat a thing. I kept thinking about the voice. Who was the woman? What did she want? What had happened to her? Who was Edward? She kept talking about him. Who was he? Was he her husband or her lover?

Later in the evening I sat by the window. The rain was falling fast. I could see the Austin outside the house. Rain was dripping down its bonnet and the windows were misty. Suddenly I felt May tapping me on the arm.

'Come on, dear,' she said, 'it's time to go. I must hurry to get the last bus.'

Was it time to go? So soon. I looked at the clock.

Yes it was late. The time had passed quickly. Now I would have to drive back in the Austin. Alone. I would have to listen to the voice again.

'Don't go on the bus,' I said to May. 'Come with me in the car. I want you to come with me. Please, May. Just once. Just tonight.'

May laughed. 'No, I'll go on the bus. I don't like that car. If I come in it tonight, you will want me to ride in it another day. I'll go on the bus.' 'I won't ask you again,' I said. 'Come with me tonight and I'll never ask you again. I'm going to get rid of the Austin. This is the last time I shall ever drive it. I'm going to sell it.'

It was true. I had made up my mind to get rid of it. But I still had to drive it home. May wouldn't come with me. She didn't understand. She didn't know about the voice. I had to drive home alone. I couldn't leave the car. I had to drive it home.

I went with May to the bus stop. It was raining hard. May put her coat over her head. I saw her get onto the last bus, then I went back to the Austin.

My hand was shaking as I opened the door and stepped into the driving seat. The inside of the car was dark and quiet. I started the engine and the car pulled away smoothly.

9

At first there was no voice. Just the sound of the engine humming softly. The rain was falling faster than ever and it was very dark. I had to drive with care. It was a bad night. The windows kept getting misty and it was hard to see the road. The smell of perfume was very strong.

Suddenly I heard something. My arms went stiff. It was the voice. The woman's voice. She was sobbing. I began to drive faster. I was afraid. I wanted to get home. The sobbing went on. On and on, sad and low.

The rain poured down. It made a thudding noise as it fell on the roof of the car. What a storm. What a night. I had to get home. The sobbing got louder. It was louder than the rain thudding on the roof. Sobbing. Crying. Where was it coming from? I was alone in the car. I must be going mad.

I put my foot down. The Austin raced along the dark road. Rain hissed on the windows. Suddenly the voice began to say my name. 'Edward. Edward. Why do you hate me? I love you, Edward.' Then it began to cry again. I couldn't stand it. I began to shout and yell. 'Shut up!' I yelled. 'Shut up! Shut up!'

It was no good. The voice went on. ‘Edward. Where are you taking me, Edward? Why are you driving so fast? Let me go home. Please, Edward. Please. I know you want to get rid of me. I know you don’t love me any more. Let me go home.’

There was nothing I could do. She wasn’t talking to me. She was talking to someone called Edward, but it wasn’t me. I kept shouting and yelling but she didn’t take any notice. I don’t think she could hear me.

I raced along the wet road. The car was going flat out. I couldn’t see where I was going and I didn’t care any more. I was mad with fear. I didn’t know what I was doing. I didn’t know where I was going.

Suddenly the woman’s voice got louder. ‘What are you doing, Edward? Why have you got that gun? Edward. Edward. Don’t shoot me, Edward! Let me get out of the car! Please, Edward. Please. Don’t kill me! Don’t kill me!’

The voice was shouting now. It was shouting in my ears. The Austin was rolling from side to side. I couldn’t keep it under control. The wheels were skidding on the wet road.

Something got hold of my arm. Someone was gripping my arm. I tried to pull my arm away but I couldn’t.

Someone was holding on to me. Suddenly the voice began to shout. 'Don't kill me, Edward! Don't kill me! You won't get away with it. Don't do it, Edward! Don't shoot me! Edw. . . .'

The voice stopped. I looked up. In the mirror I could see a face. A woman's face. It was covered with blood. A white face, covered with blood. She was behind me. She was in the back seat.

My eyes were fixed on the mirror. I felt the Austin skidding across the road. I put my foot on the brake but it didn't work. I couldn't take my eyes off the mirror. That face. The eyes looking at me. The blood.

The Austin was out of control. I couldn't stop it. I let go of the wheel and put my hands over my eyes. I crashed into a tree.

10

That is what happened. That is how I broke my back. I was in hospital for weeks. I was so ill that the doctors thought I would die. I didn't. They saved my life, but they couldn't mend my back. I will be in a wheelchair for the rest of my life.

That is my story. It's true. Every word of it. Do you believe me, or do you think I'm mad? Don't make up your mind yet. I haven't finished yet. There is something else I must tell you.

The Austin crashed. It was a bad crash. I almost died. That's how bad it was. What do you think happened to the Austin? Do you think it was smashed to bits? Do you think that it fell apart in the crash? No, it didn't.

The Austin wasn't hurt. Not at all. Not a dent. Not a scratch. It was still perfect. There wasn't a mark on it. I was almost killed but there wasn't a mark on the car. What do you make of that? I don't understand it at all.

The car was no good to me. It was sitting in the garage. A 1928 Austin in perfect condition. I couldn't drive it. I would never be able to drive it again. Never.

It was no good to me but I could get £1,000 for it. Maybe more. I needed the money. I was in a wheel-chair. I couldn't work any more. I had to sell the car.

May put an advert in the paper. AUSTIN 7, 1928, PERFECT CONDITION. RING 01 583 6261.

The next day I had a phone call. May pushed my chair cross the room and put the phone into my hand. Someone wanted to buy the Austin. It was a young man. 'Come round tomorrow,' I said. I gave him my name and address.

He was keen to buy the car. 'Thank you, Mr. Brown,' he said. 'Don't sell the Austin to anyone else. Keep it for me. My name is Jones. I'll see you tomorrow. Goodbye.'

He was going to put the phone down but I said, 'Wait. I want to ask you something. Is your name Edward?' He gave a little laugh. 'Yes,' he said, 'Edward. Edward Jones. How did you know?'

I let the phone drop from my hand.

A complete list of Spirals

Stories

Jim Alderson
Crash in the Jungle
The Witch Princess

Jan Carew
Death Comes to the Circus

Susan Duberley
The Ring

Keith Fletcher and Susan Duberley
Nightmare Lake

John Goodwin
Dead-end Job

Paul Groves
Not that I'm Work-shy
The Third Climber

Anita Jackson
The Actor
The Austin Seven
Bennet Manor
Dreams
The Ear
A Game of Life or Death
No Rent to Pay

Paul Jennings
Eye of Evil
Maggot

Margaret Loxton
The Dark Shadow

Patrick Nobes
Ghost Writer

Kevin Philbin
Summer of the Werewolf

John Townsend
Beware of the Morris Minor
Fame and Fortune
SOS

David Walke
Dollars in the Dust

Plays

Jan Carew
Computer Killer
No Entry
Time Loop

John Godfrey
When I Count to Three

Nigel Gray
An Earwig in the Ear

Paul Groves
Tell Me Where it Hurts

Barbara Mitchelhill
Punchlines
The Ramsbottoms at Home

Madeline Sotheby
Hard Times at Batwing Hall

John Townsend
Cheer and Groan
The End of the Line
Hanging by a Fred
The Lighthouse Keeper's Secret
Making a Splash
Murder at Muckleby Manor
Over and Out
Rocking the Boat
Taking the Plunge

David Walke
The Bungle Gang Strikes Again
The Good, the Bad and the Bungle
Package Holiday